Turn-Around

Originally published in the U.S.A. under the title of *Soul Surgery*.
This much revised edition first published in the United Kingdom by
The C.W. Daniel Company Limited
1 Church Path, Saffron Walden, Essex CB10 1JP, United Kingdom
© Richard & Mary-Alice Jafolla 2002
ISBN 0 85207 360 7

Produced in association with
Book Production Consultants plc,
25-27 High Street, Chesterton, Cambridge, CB4 1ND.
Designed by Marion Hughston.
Printed and bound by
St Edmundsbury Press, Bury St Edmunds, Suffolk

Richard and Mary-Alice Jafolla

Turn-Around

When your life is in crisis

Index compiled by Lyn Greenwood

SAFFRON WALDEN
THE C.W. DANIEL COMPANY LIMITED

Turn-Around

Turn-Around
Turn-Around
Turn-Around

Contents

Turn-Around

Introduction

Turn-Around

Dear Friend,

Nothing in the world is more mysterious, more complex, or more private than the landscape of your own soul. You alone traverse its peaks and valleys. You alone have travelled into its dark crevasses and across its sunlit meadows. You alone have built its prisons as well as its cathedrals.

While you may not know the route your soul has taken, whatever you are today is a direct result of that route. Right now your soul is a road atlas of your life pinpointing all the experiences, all the beliefs, all the thoughts and feelings you have gathered along the way. Many of these beliefs have caused you to detour or chase down dead ends in attempts to improve your life. And now here you are - daring to hope...just...a...bit and, yes, somewhat deterred by past failures but willing nonetheless to give it yet another try.

Your soul has its secrets. Some of these hidden thoughts and feelings are often the very obstacles preventing you from being the authentic you - the you who would experience more peace, more joy, better health, greater prosperity. Assassins who short circuit your higher self, these obstacles must be removed one by one until you are rid of them. But if you're reading this book chances are there is one *major* obstacle plaguing you today, one that has brazenly resisted every attempt to get rid of it - a crisis with such a strong hold on you and for such a long time, you wonder if you can ever be free of it? Or it might be a new situation - one that exploded into your life and whose crushing impact has scattered so much debris that you feel you have to dig out from under it before it smothers you. Maybe it's a physical challenge like heart disease, cancer or arthritis. Or it could be a substance you have allowed to gain control over you like tobacco, alcohol or some other drug, or even food! Or maybe it's a personal relationship that has become unbearable. Or have your finances collapsed? Whatever it is, this major obstacle is the one you will work on now.

Since the situation has not responded to anything you've tried so far, obviously a more radical strategy is needed. Time for a very special kind of procedure, one that offers the potential for permanent removal of the problem, leaving no pain, no scars, and no remorse. *TURN-AROUND* is such a process.

The *TURN-AROUND* process takes place in the soul, because any permanent change you make in your life can result only from changes you have first made in your soul. Obviously, this is something no one else can accomplish for you because only you have access to all the thoughts, beliefs, emotions, and memories of past experiences that are recorded in your soul.

Turn-Around

TURN-AROUND is a highly personal process - easy to understand, easy to utilize, and adapts to any lifestyle. We offer it to you in the sincere hope that it will be a blessing to you and that within its pages you will find the help you need to overcome that major challenge and turn your life around.

Our warmest wishes to you,

Richard and Mary-Alice Jafolla

Turn-Around

The Process

The Process

An ancient Hindu legend describes a time when all human beings were gods, but because they abused their divinity, Brahma, the chief god, took it away from them. Three wise holy men were called in to help Brahma decide where to hide humankind's divinity so they could never find it again.

"Let's hide it on the highest mountaintop," offered the first holy man.

"No, humans are very resourceful. Eventually someone will climb up there and find it. Instead, let's hide it at the bottom of the deepest sea," suggested the second holy man. But they realized in time someone would discover it there as well.

"Let's bury it deep in the Earth," said the third holy man. But they all realized there, too, it would one day be found.

After much thought and deliberation they decided to bury divinity deep within each person. "No one will ever think to look for it there!" they exclaimed. And there it has remained ever since.

The Heart Of TURN-AROUND

We explore the outer reaches of space, the unbelievable depths of the oceans, the very bowels of the Earth, we search far and wide to "find ourselves". But how few of us ever think to look inside. Our divinity is deeply hidden in every human heart where it waits to be discovered, ever ready to provide all the answers and guidance and solace we will ever need.

Only when we're armed with the knowledge that we have a divine presence within us will we dare to step out of the "but-I'm-only-human" mindset and identify with the dimension that does not deal on that level - a *higher* dimension. *The solution to a problem is never found on the level of the problem itself.* It is found on a higher level, where all answers and all possibilities await. The more we can identify with this level, the easier life becomes. This is the heart of *TURN-AROUND*.

Does This Mean We Need "God" On This Trip?

Before addressing that critical question, let's take a slight detour to define our terms and to distinguish between "religion" and "spirituality".

We are all spiritual but not all of us are religious. Spirituality, as we are using the term in this book, refers to our awareness of our relationship with a higher power that resides in each of us. Spirituality relies on *inner* knowledge and *inner* feelings, and so each of us expresses his or her spirituality in an absolutely unique manner. Religion, on the other hand, is a set of formalized beliefs created by an individual or group and is practised by the members of that group. Religions are constructed on frameworks of outer rules and tenets.

Getting back to whether we need "God" on this trip, the answer hinges on how we're defining God. You'll have to use your own innate wisdom to make the final determination yourself. But here's our reasoning: When faced with situations that seem threatening or even tragic, our human tendency is to allow the mere appearances to influence us in a negative way. As a result, we anxiously scramble around for the solution amidst the very chaos of the situation. But (at the risk of being redundant) *the solution to a problem is never found on the level of the problem.* How could it be? For example, if you walked into quicksand, the more you struggled, the deeper you would be sucked into it. The trick to keeping out of trouble in quicksand is first to stop struggling - that only makes it worse. (Dare we say it again? *The solution to a problem is never found on the level of the problem.*) When you stop struggling, your natural buoyancy keeps you afloat. But then what? Then you need someone positioned higher than you are and standing on firmer footing to lend you a hand and pull you out.

Okay, so far so good. Now, how does this apply to you? If you feel you are in an impossible situation without the ability to resolve it yourself, doesn't it make sense that you have to turn elsewhere for help? And help can only come from a power "higher" than you yourself - a *Higher Power* - one transcending the human level of the situation. If your life is currently mired in the quicksand of an addiction or an illness or financial crisis or poverty or whatever, why not look for the *highest* power you can find? An awareness of this higher power can help you, but...BUT...this knowledge cannot be of any help to you while you're struggling and thrashing about in the problem. And, too, keep in mind the Hindu legend: you don't have to look "upward" to contact this power; you'll find it available if you look "inward". The secret of *TURN-AROUND* is its reliance on working with this creative force *already* part of you, part of us all. What lies in our past or what lies in our future is insignificant compared to what lies within us.

One God, Many Names

Higher Power, Inner Wisdom, Nature, Cosmic Mind, Supreme Being, the Infinite, Universal Intelligence, Allah, Creator, and a multitude of others - the power most people refer to as "God" is called by many names and is conceptualized in many ways.

You have your own concept of God, your own belief or non-belief regarding a supreme power, and it's certainly not for us to define for you what that is. But the fundamental tenet of *TURN-AROUND* holds that God - whatever "God" is - is not something to be worshipped, rather *it is a principle to be lived - a presence dwelling within each of us. You can never be separated from this presence because you are an expression of it.* So rather than praying to this power to do something to help us, we *allow* it to work through us as a living principle. Because this invisible source is in each of us, it supports each of us, and benefits our lives to the degree we are in synch with it. When navigating a river, we make the most progress when we paddle *with* the flow.

The Promise Of TURN-AROUND

So often we look for outside answers to inside "problems", when all the while there is an inner wisdom that remains untapped. No matter what your own situation appears to be, the *real* problem is seldom the one you see. The real problem is your inability or your subconscious unwillingness to allow this inner wisdom to unfold its plan through you.

It is human nature to see a problematic situation as a set of circumstances "out there" interfering with your happiness - with your desire to be rich or not to be poor, to be respected or not to be scorned, to be loved or not to be ignored, to be...or not to be. So you find yourself asking your friends, your neighbours, your loved ones for answers. You may even seek professional counselling if your pain is severe enough. "What do you think I should do?" You can end up with all kinds of advice but still with no answer to the question, "What is the best thing for me?" Without involving your inner wisdom in the decision, you are simply rolling dice because there is a higher, broader plan at work.

Right now it may seem to the contrary, but the fact is you live in a supportive universe whose benefits are available to you at all times. *You enjoy these benefits when you become aware of them and allow them access into your life.* This is one of the foundation stones upon which *TURN-AROUND* is built. If you can accept this basic premise and keep it uppermost in your mind, you will experience surprising changes. If initially you are having trouble accepting this basic premise, we urge you to stay with *TURN-AROUND* anyway because even when practised half-heartedly the seven steps can still help.

Turn-Around

The seven *TURN-AROUND* steps do not *make* something happen. In truth you can't "make" anything happen. Sure, you can sometimes manipulate people, circumstances, and events to give yourself temporary comfort and the illusion that you are in charge. Trouble is, the only glue to hold them all together is the strength of your own will. If you let your guard down even for a minute the same people, circumstances and events revert to their former levels and you have to round them up and glue them back together again. So you can see it's a continuous process requiring an enormous amount of effort - one that eventually wears you out!

TURN-AROUND, on the other hand, rather than trying to "make" something happen, frees up your soul and *prepares* it to accept the right things when they present themselves.

This is a short book - the seven steps of *TURN-AROUND* are brief and to the point. You won't have to waste time reading pages and pages of theoretical ideas or spend agonizing months or years on self-analysis. You can enter into this process with the hope-filled feeling that help is here at last. If you are willing to follow the seven steps and not skip over anything or slacken your commitment, you will be pleased at how your life will look and feel in the near future.

Turn-Around

Instructions

Turn-Around

Instructions

Achieving a goal is not the only reward for our industrious work. The journey itself is part of the reward! Let's take exercise as an example. Perfect health can be a goal and one of the paths to good health is exercise. Yet the immediate reward of exercise is not perfect health. Fitness is a journey, not a destination. The treasure lies in the exercising itself, and every time we do it we are rewarded.

We can desire more money or a better relationship or physical healing for ourselves or a loved one, but in a sense these are narrow goals leading at best to narrow rewards. Expanding our awareness beyond a limited goal will help us achieve not only the goal but the broader inner peace and soul satisfaction we are actually craving. For example, you may want a new car. There are many ways to get a car. You can save your money and buy one or you can get a car loan or lease a car or rent one. You can win a car in a lottery or be given a car (you can even steal a car!). In the end, all you will have is a car.

But if you expand your consciousness past the specific desire for a car to include prosperity in general, your whole life will experience greater riches, including a car. When you expand your field of vision, that specific item you have been focusing on will still be in view, but so will lots of other things, tangible as well as intangible.

Simple Is Not Always Easy

The *TURN-AROUND* steps can seem deceptively simple because cooperating with the life force is simple. (But "simple" is not necessarily "easy".)

1 Begin by quickly reading through the entire book to gain an overview of the process. Don't spend lots of time in any chapter trying to pull all of the essence out of it; you'll do that later. For now, just read the book at a steady pace. (The seven steps of *TURN-AROUND* are a continuum, a progression - more like floating on an ocean current rather than simply riding an individual wave.)

2 Now go back to Step One and proceed to work through the seven steps, one chapter at a time, systematically applying each chapter to your specific situation. Read each chapter with an open mind, allowing the ideas to find their way into your heart.

3 After you have thoroughly read a chapter, you will be asked to take some steps - *Soul Steps* - to reinforce what you've read and to "make it your own". It is here in

these *Soul Steps* that your soul will be doing its work, making the progress that will lead to your success. That's why it is crucial you give these *Soul Steps* your very best.

4 Proceed deliberately. Be patient and *do not hurry*. The ultimate goal of an out-of-shape man may be to compete in a twenty-six mile marathon. If he can't run that distance now, as long as he runs as far as he can each day, he will eventually become strong enough to go the full distance. Like the runner, as long as you are striving to improve you are improving. It's possible you may experience temporary set-backs or periods when you see no improvement, but these are usually times when your consciousness - your soul - is busily working to accept a new concept. So be patient and hang in there. (Does the farmer dig up the seeds to see if they are growing?) Trust the process.

5 Throughout your turn-around process you will be asked to suspend your normal reactions, to do some about-faces to your preconceived mindsets. (After all, this is a "turn-around".) Again, trust the process. Your normal reactions have contributed to the predicament you find yourself in, so suspending your normal reactions may be the very strategy needed if you are serious about changing your life.

6 Lastly, and most importantly, it is usually best to work alone. *TURN-AROUND* is such a personal process that it should not be shared with anyone unless he or she is *very* close to you and is sincerely interested in your spiritual well-being. The soul has special secrets and those secrets are for you alone to discover. If you feel you must share them, be sure it is with someone who has your absolute best interests at heart. After all, if you were going to climb a mountain, would you do it with someone afraid of heights? If you need someone to journey with you to new spiritual heights, be sure to choose a partner who can see at least as high as you can.

Making New And Better

Now here's some good news! Even when you work alone you are not alone. The spirit of life is always with you because you are part of life. The wisdom is within, available at all times to guide you and to help you. This inner wisdom lives in you as your own personal inner wisdom, a power you can count on because its nature is to continuously make new and better. The implication of this is awesome; "what was" does not have to be "what is". Things *can* be different. The creative process of the universe is designed to create. It is we who try to hold it in the ruts of the past. Just being aware of this creative process opens the way for some major transformations to take place - especially when we realize that we are co-creators with this force. It cannot work alone, it can only work through us. However, if we are closed to the possibility of any positive changes, the process cannot work.

But when you are open to changes, when you are in tune and in synch with your inner wisdom, things will begin working in a way that feels "right". You will view each event and person as an integral part of some greater plan, and be able to perceive them as participants in this greater plan. The more aware you are of a higher presence and power in your life, the more clearly you recognize some sort of order is taking place. And with this recognition comes progress. If a million pounds were deposited in your bank account without your knowledge, the money would do you no good. Only with the *recognition* would come the benefit.

Okay. Ready? Then let's go now to the first step of your *TURN-AROUND.*

Turn-Around

Step One -
AWARENESS

Step One - AWARENESS

No matter what we think we want, our real need is to become more aware of our relationship with our source.

In the dead of winter a man sets out from Canada to drive to sunny Miami. The further he drives, the colder it gets. He begins taking jumpers and jackets out of his suitcase, hoping to remedy the situation by putting on more and more clothing. But with each passing mile the temperature drops even lower. He stops to buy warmer clothing, but no matter how much he wraps up he cannot get warm. Something is wrong - he clearly has a problem. Yet his only hope of solving it lies with his first becoming aware he *has* a problem. Only when he realizes he is driving *north* instead of south can he take any steps to change things. Unfortunately, once our man realizes his mistake, he begins to berate himself for his "stupidity", his poor choices of roads, his worthlessness as a navigator. He pulls into a service station on the motorway and spends considerable time trying to figure out where he went wrong. But at this point does it really matter *why* he drove in the wrong direction? What's the difference? It has nothing to do with the solution. The important move is to face the car in a new direction and start back. Digging up the past to see why he drove north instead of south is a waste of time and energy. His first question should be, "Where am I now?" Only when he answers this can he concentrate on, "Where do I go from here?"

We concocted this story simply to illustrate a point. Digging up the past and rehashing who's right or wrong or who did what to whom or, "Why am I in this mess?" will not move you in the direction you want to be heading. The first question in any difficult situation is always, "Where am I *now?*"

Taking It Up A Notch

We'll call *Where am I?* Level One. Only when you answer this can you concentrate on the next level, the higher level: *Where do I go from here?* Here's another analogy that may help to explain this next level.

You feel hungry and so you go into a restaurant and look over the menu. Your mouth waters for soup, chicken salad and baked potato, and apple pie and coffee. You tell the waitress that's what you want. But is it *really* the soup and chicken salad and potatoes and apple pie and coffee you want? Not really. Your *real* desire, the underlying need, is for nourishment for your cells. That's why you are hungry and that's why you are eating. You eat because the hundred trillion cells of your body need raw material and, until these cells are nourished, you will remain hungry. So, in this case, *Where am I?* can be answered by: *I am hungry.* The next level - *Where do I go from here?* - identifies the real need. In this case the real need is *nourishment for the cells.*

Let's apply this to your own life. You may desire a new car or a new relationship or a physical or emotional healing or the breaking of a harmful habit or the rekindling of a relationship - that's what you *think* you want. That's obvious. But if you could see beyond the hunger to the need, you would discover what you really want is a greater awareness of the power that created you and sustains you. In fact, if the road does not eventually lead to a greater awareness of this universal presence, just as if the food you eat doesn't lead to greater nourishment for your cells, the hunger will persist and you will try to fill the hunger with more cars or bigger homes or shinier rings or more glamorous mates or drugs or sex or whatever. You will try to fill the void with "things".

Any dissatisfaction you feel when a problem rears its ugly head is not from being too poor or unloved or sick or addicted or whatever else you are wrestling with. The dissatisfaction is actually a "divine dissatisfaction" deep in your soul - the discontent of not feeling more of the presence of the creative power that moulds this universe and has created you and offers you its attributes. You may think the answer to your problem is to get what you want: *"If I could only get a job, any job, I'd be happy." "If I could only find someone who loves me everything would be all right." "If I could just get rid of this pain life would be wonderful." "There's nothing wrong with me that a hundred thousand pounds couldn't fix." "If I could only stop drinking!"*

The biggest lie you will ever tell yourself is, *"When I get what I want I'll be happy"*, because what you are *really* yearning for is to reconnect with the power that runs this universe. What you *really* want is a greater awareness of this presence. It's actually a yearning to come home again. Like a portable power tool that must be returned to its charger to regain and maintain its power, we all yearn to reconnect with our source. No matter what we *think* we want, what we *really* want is to feel fully at one with this source again.

To Bring This Back Full Circle

With the recognition of your hunger for more of a spiritual awareness comes the realization that it's not important where the problem came from, nor how long it has been in your life. What is important is that you can begin where you are to do something about it. Like the man driving to Miami, your first step is to identify where you are right now. Don't allow yourself to get detoured - stay on the straight and narrow with this one. In the overall scheme of things, it is not important where the problem came from.

That said, let's now take a step sideways. There's no searching for a solution if you're not perfectly clear about what you are trying to solve. What is it in your life you want to change? Identify clearly what your challenge is. Go past the superficial and get to the underlying need. In the case of the man travelling from Canada, he thought his problem was a lack of warm clothing, but this was only treating the symptom. The real need was a new direction.

Time out! Not so fast! You've just finished saying my real goal is not what I think it is, that what I really want is to feel at one with my source. Now you're telling me I have to identify a specific goal?

Yes, indeed, reconnecting with your inner wisdom is your real desire. But this goal is often too nebulous, too fluid, too slippery to get your arms around, and it would take a gigantic leap of faith to go from the pain you are now experiencing to adopting that attitude. So the easiest place to start is with your most immediate challenge. If you're like most people, the physical or psychological pain you are experiencing is too big a hurdle to jump before sprinting straight to the finish line. To use the exercise analogy once more, running in the Olympic Marathon may be your ultimate goal but your immediate challenge is to get in shape. You may have to begin by running a single mile or maybe even a few hundred yards. In striving to run your first mile your ultimate goal of completing the marathon will always be in your mind for sure, but the more immediate need is to run that first mile.

We humans have a hierarchy of needs. Our need for food and shelter precedes our need for just about anything else including spiritual fulfilment. We need to feel secure in having a roof over our heads and enough to eat before we will venture out to fulfil other needs. And so we'll be hard-pressed to make the effort to improve our spiritual life when most of our time is spent looking for something to eat and somewhere to sleep. In other words, it's tough to be a saint if you are hungry and homeless!

In much the same way, your present need to rid your life of whatever serious physical and/or emotional challenge is facing you is getting in the way of your expressing the unique and authentic person you really are. It's interfering with your relationship with what created you. So while keeping in mind the ultimate goal of feeling fully at one with your source, it's first things first. Getting rid of your present crisis is where you will have to start your spiritual odyssey.

Turn-Around

Awareness - SOUL STEPS

Awareness - SOUL STEPS

No one wants to run full speed in the dark. Shedding light on your challenge will allow you to move ahead with enthusiasm and confidence.

Clearly identifying your challenge is obviously a critical first step. Precisely why are you reading this book? If you don't know where you are, it's impossible to know how to get to where you want to go. Ever get lost in a big city? Isn't the first thing you do to look at the road names to determine where you are? Only when you know where you are can you begin finding out how to get to where you want to go.

1 Because clarifying your immediate challenge is an important step, take some time to consider it before writing your answer. Here are some examples to help you:

> **My challenge is:** *I keep choosing men who are emotionally unavailable.*
> **I want to change:** *the belief that I'm not worthy of a healthy relationship.*

> **My challenge is:** *I don't have enough money.*
> **I want to change:** *the feeling that I don't deserve to be prosperous.* Or, *the feeling that I'm a loser.*

Now it's time to write your own. Be specific and keep it simple.

My challenge is:

_____

_____

_____

_____

I want to change:

_____

_____

_____

_____

2 A cosmic intelligence in you responds when you acknowledge it. You communicate with this intelligence through an inner awareness, and probably the best way to establish this communication is by sitting calmly and opening yourself to the wisdom of this intelligence. The most common name for this activity is meditation, but

don't let the word scare you - there's really nothing strange about it.

Before determining what meditation is, here are a few things meditation isn't. Meditation is *NOT*:

- a "high"
- an escape from reality
- self-hypnosis
- prayer

Meditation *IS* the conscious direction of one's attention to the inner self. It allows you to get in touch with that wisdom deep within you that can always be relied upon to let you know what to do. Because it is the quickest and surest way to increase your awareness, regular meditation should be an important part of your daily activity.

Is meditation an altered state of consciousness? Yes, sort of, but then if you've ever driven on a motorway for a few hours and have suddenly realized you've missed your exit because you'd been daydreaming, that, too, was an altered state of consciousness. Or how about being "taken away" by a beautiful piece of music? Or so fully concentrating on a mathematical problem so that you were unaware of anything else going on around you?

How To Meditate

To become aware of your soul's needs, set aside time each day for regular, quiet meditation. There is no trick to meditation. Just find a comfortable chair in a quiet spot, close your eyes and sit in silence. Don't *try* to think of anything, but if a thought floats through your mind, simply observe it. Do not analyze it or try to get rid of it.

One good meditative technique and one that works for most people is to simply observe your breathing. That's all. Simply become consciously aware of your breathing. As you do this, keep breathing naturally. In...and out. In...and out. In...and out. Don't change the rhythm in any way. Merely be aware of your breathing. Concentrate on it. Actually experience it. This works well to keep idle thoughts at bay.

For the first week or so it may be difficult to sit quietly for even a brief time. Your mind, like an inquisitive monkey, may jump from thought to thought, rebelling at the unfamiliar stillness. But keep at it. It won't be long before the hyperactive monkey settles down and you are savouring this quiet time.

Begin with one five-minute session in the morning and another at night. Eventually you can increase these sessions to twenty minutes or as many minutes as you feel comfortable with. In time, the right answers and the right direction for you will come forth from your own inner spirit, for it is most assuredly there waiting to help you. Remember, this is *NOT* a time to think about a problem or a solution, definitely not. On the contrary, *it's a time to simply sit and be receptive* - not consciously thinking any particular thoughts. So don't expect answers necessarily to emerge during your meditation, they seldom do. Rather, they often surface when you least expect it. Sometimes it will be a spontaneous illumination, like the light bulbs shown in cartoons to signify a bright idea. Or the answer may appear in the form of a dream or while you're daydreaming. It may come in the form of a feeling that slowly overwhelms you and suddenly you know what to do. You may hear words you've heard before or read something you've read before, but which this time seem different and new and directed especially at *you* as if you've heard them or read them for the very first time. Whatever way these messages appear, do pay attention to them. They are gifts to you from the universe and arise out of your own inner awareness of what's *really* best for you.

Turn-Around

Step Two -
BLESSING

Step Two - BLESSING

A problem has only one dimension - itself.
An opportunity has infinite possibilities.

The fans in the stands were going wild with excitement. First the green-shirted team scored and their fans screamed approval. Then the blue-shirted team scored and their fans screamed their approval. Back and forth it went with one team scoring and then the other until finally, just before time ran out, the green-shirted team scored the game-winning goal. The game was over.

Bedlam broke out among the green-shirted supporters. They mobbed their team, jumping up and down in excitement, laughing and hugging each other in glee.

On the blue side there was only silence, sadness and a few tears. The players sat on their bench dejected, heads hanging down in utter misery.

Was the outcome of the game good or bad? It depended on whether you were wearing green or blue. In actuality, the outcome of the game was neutral. It was neither good nor bad *but thinking made it so.*

All events are neutral. If they were not then everyone would have exactly the same feelings felt with the same intensity about all events. But that's far from the case.

Another example: What's your reaction when you read about someone's death in the obituaries? Unless you knew the person, most of the time you are completely neutral. Yet the person's death has brought great sorrow to those who loved him and possibly some joy to someone who hated him. What is the truth about the person's death? It was neither good nor bad, neither negative nor positive, *but thinking made it so.*

Events Are Neutral

Any situation confronting you - whether you label it "negative" or "positive", whether in your body or in your outer affairs - *any* situation contains the seed of a blessing. It doesn't matter how negative it seems to you or to your friends or to your doctor or to your lawyer or to your psychiatrist or to your marriage counsellor or to anyone else, there is a blessing here for you. That's why it is risky to draw conclusions from the "appearance" of things, because you are interpreting appearances exclusively with your five senses. Why base any judgements on data supplied by such limited and fallible instruments?

"Negative" and "positive" are constructs of your own mind, which basically means all events are neutral. You decide if they are "negative" or "positive", depending on the effect you feel they have on your life. The event itself, however, is neither negative nor positive - it just *is*. It's neutral. To the picnickers the rain was negative, to the farmer it was positive. To the little boy, bringing home a stray puppy was a positive, but to his mother it was a negative. All events in your life are neutral. It is you who brands them with a negative or positive and decides the extent of the impact they will have on you. What happens *to* you is not nearly as important as what happens *through* you. The circumstances that impact your life can't possibly be controlled. Governmental decisions, the actions of your family members, the price of crude oil, the weather, your car breaking down - an infinite number of variables continually impact your life and it's impossible to control them. But what happens *within* you as you deal with those circumstances is always your decision and therefore *can* be controlled. (Right now such control may seem an unrealistic goal, but as you move through *TURN-AROUND* the seven steps are going to make it more possible for you to exercise this kind of control.)

Search For The Blessing

Several years ago a couple we know (and this is a true story) left their jobs and invested all of their savings into building and selling small sailing boats - a long-time dream of theirs. Two years later, deeply in debt and barely making ends meet, they were devastated when a large boat dealership opened less than a mile away. With their little capital and poor cash flow, how could they ever successfully compete with the "big boys"? Seeing a monster problem ready to swallow them up, they were ready to pack it in. But in a moment of calm reflection, they were able to shift their perception of the situation and an exciting idea promptly popped into their minds. They saw a blessing - an opportunity - in the midst of the crisis! Reminding themselves that their area was drawing more and more tourists, they came up with a plan to rent out boats rather than sell them. It was the best move they ever made, and today they own the largest boat rental business in the area. Hidden within the crisis they faced had been a great blessing for them. By knowing there was a blessing *somewhere*, they were able to shift their perspective and "think out of the box". Shifting their perspective, they opened themselves to an exciting new possibility and their life is now so much easier.

Change One Gear - Any Gear

Do you believe the events of your life have a power of their own - a power to overwhelm you? They don't.

Turn-Around

Remember, all events are neutral and are subject to *your* thoughts about them.

Your task, then - are you ready for this? - is to start forgetting about how things look, to stop making decisions about situations based only on how they *appear.* Instead, begin training yourself to look for the blessing in *every* situation. Yes, it's a big job and it requires constant attention. It might even require thinking and reacting one hundred and eighty degrees from your present methods, but it is absolutely worth every bit of the effort you give it.

What? Bless my wife for the pain she's caused our family with her drinking? You've got to be joking! No, we're not joking. No one can ruin your life without your permission. When you change your thoughts and feelings, you don't have to change your situation! It changes automatically because your involvement, the energy you bring to it, is a critical part of the mix. When that changes, the mix changes.

Imagine for a moment a room filled with a hundred interconnected gears all involved in the turning of a huge Ferris wheel. When any one gear turns, obviously, all gears turn (since they are interconnected) and, ultimately, the Ferris wheel turns. If you wanted the Ferris wheel to change speed or direction you would only have to change the speed or size or direction of one gear, any gear, and *all* gear movements would be affected. That one change in just that one gear would affect the speed and/or the direction the Ferris wheel turned. All you would have to do is change *one* gear - *any* gear - and all gears would be forced to change and the Ferris wheel would be affected accordingly.

Think of the attitude you bring to your specific challenge as one "gear" - an extremely critical one - that is affecting the situation you find yourself in. When you change *your* attitude, every aspect of your present situation will change.

This is one of the main reasons why programmes that support the families of alcoholics, are so successful. They teach you how to detach from the situation, how to shift gears in your own life and see the behaviour of your loved one in a different light.

Untangle Yourself

When you bless a situation you untangle yourself from its clutches. The multi-tentacled octopus wrapped around you immediately loosens its grip because it was *your* belief that gave it its full power. You no longer have to struggle and strain. Instead, you can swim along with the tide, observing events as they unfold, aware that as long as you keep in touch with your inner wisdom, the blessings will surface.

Turn-Around

So isn't it time to stop classifying certain circumstances and events as problems or as obstacles. Understandably, this may be contrary to the way you normally look at things but, before you discard the idea, force yourself to try it just this once. Begin seeing your "problems" as challenges, as situations providing you with the opportunity to grow. Does a body-builder resent those heavy weights he lifts in the gym? No, because he doesn't think of them as "problems" or as "obstacles" blocking his progress. He's grateful to them for giving him a chance to gain strength. The frail boy lifts hundreds of pounds of bar-bells so he can develop his muscles. Some people would curse the weights, seeing only hundreds of hours of sweat and strain, fatigue, pain, muscle strains, and injuries. The young man blesses them because what he sees is a new and better body.

Loneliness, poverty, sickness - these are some of the challenges that can force people to grow. Bless these challenges because, no matter how else they may affect you, they give you an opportunity for soul growth.

The Only Way Out

Are you reluctant to bless a situation you abhor because you're afraid this will attach it more firmly to you? Quite the opposite is true. The only way out of every unwanted situation is to love your way out. Bless and be grateful for whatever is showing you your present limitations. Give it a try. (Don't you bless the mirror that shows you the piece of spinach stuck on your front tooth?) By blessing your present situation you admit to yourself there is an area of your life that needs attention, and the person or event involved has shown you what it is. The circumstance itself is then detached from your life. If you stay caught up in a problem, you can only rise to the height of the problem. By blessing it, you've transmuted it from a problem to an opportunity. A problem has only one dimension: itself. Ah, but an opportunity? An opportunity has *infinite* possibilities. (Now, that's worth repeating: *A problem has only one dimension: itself. An opportunity has infinite possibilities.*)

The Power To Judge

In the classic fairy tale *Beauty and the Beast,* a young maiden is held captive by a horrible-looking beast who loves her and asks her to marry him. The maiden is repulsed by the beast and adamantly refuses. Yet day after day he follows her around, persisting in his proposal, and she is just as persistent in her refusal. She pines away for her freedom, despairing over never being able to escape from the repugnant beast. Alas, there finally comes a time when, resigned to her fate, she opens her heart to the pathetic creature and, in doing so, is overwhelmed by compassion for him. She consents to marry him, whereupon he is immediately transformed into a handsome prince who takes her to his splendid kingdom where they live happily ever after.

The ability to bless a situation is one of the greatest gifts you possess, and is not to be taken lightly. Blessing something or someone will transform *you*, and in so doing change every aspect of your life. You have a free will that allows *you* the choice of seeing an opportunity or seeing only gloom and doom. The direction your judgement takes rests completely in your own hands - or, rather, in your own soul. Transport yourself to new spiritual and mental and physical plateaus or plunge yourself into the depths of loneliness, poverty, hatred and sickness. *You* decide.

If there is a persistent challenge following you around, don't run away from it any longer. Stop, confront the "beast" face to face, and know within even the most negative appearance, exists the seed of an unexpected blessing. Don't waste another precious minute - make way for the next exciting chapter of your life by blessing that situation now!

Turn-Around

Blessing -
SOUL STEPS

Blessing - SOUL STEPS

Visible light, in other words what we can see with our eyes, is part of something called the electromagnetic spectrum. This spectrum ranges in wavelengths from unimaginably tiny cosmic waves to radio waves that are thousands of miles in length. Yet in this immense spectrum the human eye can see only between infrared and ultraviolet, a little over one per cent! (That's like being able to hear only one note on a piano.)

Yet in spite of such physical limitations, many of us continue to feel we can rely on our senses to fully understand our world. "Seeing is believing" we say. But is it? Is it possible the way you're seeing your situation is not the way it *really* is? You may not think it possible now, but how about just opening yourself to the *possibility* of the possibility?

1 Consider in what way(s) your particular situation might turn out to be a blessing to you. For a few minutes put aside your old thinking about the challenge and allow your inner wisdom to come up with something new. See it in a fresh way from a different angle. The *Mona Lisa* is a dirty old canvas when viewed from the back. From the front, it's a masterpiece. It all

depends on how you choose to look at it.

Write a paragraph or two on this.

_____

_____

_____

_____

_____

_____

2 If you can't bless your situation, "fake it until you make it". This may sound like strange advice but it's not. When we "fake it", when we force ourselves to consistently think and act in a certain way, we begin creating new neural pathways, new ways for the brain to process information. By consciously acting "as if", we will begin accepting those new thoughts and actions as real.

a) **Create a *meaningful* blessing you can repeat whenever you think of the situation troubling you.**

Make it short - something easy to remember. There's a story about a positive-thinking boy who, when confronted with a room stacked six feet high in horse manure, exclaimed happily, "There has to be a pony in here *somewhere!*"

Here are some examples that might help you:

Something totally unexpected and wonderful will come of this.

There's a blessing in this for me.

My blessing: ——————————————

——————————————

——————————————

b) **Memorize this blessing. Say it often throughout the day.**

3 Having difficulty blessing someone? The following suggestions may help.

Set aside a definite time each day to actively bless the situation or person troubling you.

a) Try to see the invisible "sign" hanging around this person's neck that reads "Please Love Me". Bring this image into your quiet time each day. See that sign blinking brightly - *Please love me...Please love me...Please love me* - and know his or her need for love is always there, no matter how successfully the person has been able to hide it.

b) Envisage the person as an infant. See the sweet, innocent baby he or she once was. It's easy to love a baby. The more clearly you can see this person as a baby, the more easy it will be to bless him or her.

4 Finally, **take a Blessings Inventory!** When was the last time you listed the things in your life you were thankful for? You've probably been so involved with your present challenge that you may have overlooked the blessings in your life. Take time now to actively and consciously appreciate these blessings. They could be your children, spouse, friends, your sense of humour, your home, or even your favourite armchair or your favourite ice-cream flavour. Make a list now of every thing in your life that you are thankful for.

Turn-Around

Step Three - COMMITMENT

Step Three - COMMITMENT

Knowing what needs to be done and actually doing it are two shores separated by a river of lethargy. Commitment is the bridge that joins them.

"This day we sailed on." Day after day, month after month Christopher Columbus's daily log entry was the same: "This day we sailed on." Despite such horrendous conditions that the crew was threatening mutiny, the Italian navigator never wavered in his conviction that a New World lay on the other side of the Atlantic. A man obsessed by his quest, his course was set, and for him there were no options but to sail on. Columbus discovered the New World because he never lost his unshakable commitment to reaching his goal.

No great deeds are ever completed without great commitment, for commitment is fundamental to any meaningful change. Commitment, therefore, is the third step of *TURN-AROUND.* We have to *want* to change our lives before we will ever take the first steps to do so. If we are not motivated to act, there will be little or no action.

Every challenge presents two choices for dealing with it - two separate voices vying for our attention - and the choice we make is critical. We can listen to our inner wisdom that will reveal the truth of the situation, gently urging us to face the challenge and dare us to take action. Or, we can tune into the noisy chatter of our senses that gathers input only from outer appearances and jeers at us: "This is incurable", or, "Just accept your fate", or, "You'll always be an alcoholic", or, "You're stupid". The voice we listen to will determine the effect of the challenge on us. If we listen to the cacophony of our own sensory impressions or the negative attitude of well-meaning friends or the pessimistic pronouncements from the news media and voices of the world in general, we can easily be convinced we are victims at the mercy of such "bad luck".

If, on the other hand, we connect with the intelligence within us that tells us the desire to change our lives is really the universe prodding us to express more and more of our true nature, then the "insurmountable problem" will begin to shrink and take on a different appearance. Ultimately, it will serve as a stepping-stone to something positive and satisfying.

Unless we are strongly committed to overcoming a situation - to improving our lives - we run the risk of giving up before we have reached the final goal. Without commitment we are like a powerful generator waiting for the switch to be flicked on: rich in potential but incapable of activating it. Yet even commitment is worthless unless we know what it is we want to do!

Meaningful Goals

Before you can make a meaningful commitment, you must first have a firm goal in mind - not only firm, but rational and reachable. A frail, five-foot-tall woman may want to play professional rugby, but how rational and reachable is that? Does she *really* believe she can compete with six-foot-six-inch, three-hundred-pound men?

The *meaningful* goals in life *are* attainable. Things like loving and being able to accept love, feeling genuine joy, experiencing inner peace, enjoying abundant prosperity - these are the attitudes and beliefs that bring us great happiness. These are the meaningful goals you may feel your present situation is blocking.

Use Your Imagination

Use the most creative of your mind powers - *imagination* - to help you envisage and feel a successful outcome to a challenge you are facing. If you cannot, all of your efforts are handicapped before you even begin. The great golfer, Tiger Woods, envisages the outcome of each shot before he hits the ball. By consciously directing your mind to hold a definite, firmly pictured outcome, you will be subconsciously directing your life toward attaining that outcome. Imagination can awaken your inner forces. It can activate latent powers that would otherwise never emerge because imagination carries with it feelings and emotions that spur you into action. Of this you can be sure: *when you mentally "see" a goal, when you can viscerally "feel" the goal, the mysterious inner resources of your soul will work single-mindedly toward the fulfilment of that goal.* There's no such thing as a free lunch, so naturally you have to put forth some effort, but if you are able to *see and feel* your goal as already reached, the hidden forces in you rally to move you toward it.

Consider a man walking in the desert - lost, tired and badly in need of water. As long as he sees only sand dunes, it is very difficult for him to stay motivated to keep walking. He's morbidly aware of the heat, his thirst, his burning feet, his weary body. But no matter how hot or tired or thirsty or depressed he is, let him reach the top of a dune and spot an oasis in the distance, and his motivation to continue is immediately restored. Suddenly the heat, the thirst and the weariness disappear. His commitment is now single-minded. Now he can *see* the palm trees and the pond, he can *feel* the shade and the water, and all of his energies will be directed toward reaching his goal.

Turn-Around

You've been "thirsting", friend, but there's an oasis on the horizon. Begin to see your goal clearly and distinctly, get in touch with how it will feel. Fix it in your mind and keep it there. Every time you think of your situation, see yourself as having already attained a positive outcome. Continue to think of yourself in exactly the way you want to be and you will be given the impetus to attain it. *You cannot help becoming whatever you truly believe about yourself.*

An Important Step

A firm commitment, then, is a vital step in your turn-around. Great deeds need great commitments to those deeds. In order to express the greatness and the splendour within yourself you need commitment to it. Shallow commitment = limited action. Limited action = incomplete results. You've probably had enough incomplete results in your life. Resolve to let this time be different. Make a strong commitment...now.

Turn-Around

Commitment - SOUL STEPS

Commitment - SOUL STEPS

K nowing what needs to be done and actually doing it are two shores separated by a river of lethargy. Commitment is the bridge that joins them.

Commitment is putting "feet" on your prayers. It's fine to pray but don't stop there. Put some action behind your prayers. Let's face it, a desire without "feet" is a dead end, a dream that will evanesce into the nothingness all dreams become when not translated into action. Commitment is the gear-stick in your car - you may have a powerful engine racing at full throttle, plenty of petrol, and know where you want to go, but unless you shift into gear, you'll stay in the driveway.

So what can you do to strengthen your commitment? A good place to start is with your focus. What you see is what you get (and what you've got is what you've seen!). Focusing on the past is like driving your car while looking into the rear-view mirror. But focus on the future, on your goal, and that will motivate you to get there.

So often people's inability to reach a goal is simply because they have never had a clear vision of exactly what their goal is.

"I'm very dissatisfied with where I am and I'd like to buy an airline ticket."

"Yes, sir, where would you like to go?"

"I'm praying for guidance."

How can the person ever reach his destination if he doesn't know where he wants to go? So often our inability to reach our goal is due to our having no clear goal to begin with.

Do you have a *clear* vision of what you want? The clearer your vision of what you want, the more chance you have of fulfilling it. Don't let your present vision blur it (and it will if you're not careful), because your present vision is the habitual vision you've been seeing when you think about your present challenge. The old vision will hang on unless you *consciously* make a substitution every time it looms up.

1 Now is the time to answer some important questions, the first being the most important - a very simple question, but loaded!

What do I really want?

Why are you reading this book? What specific changes do you want to create in your life? Easy enough, right? Or is it? Are you like the person at the ticket counter who just wants to be somewhere else or feel some way else? Or is what you want clear enough in your mind that you can write it out? It's best to list what changes you want to make and then pick the one single statement that best represents this desire.

For example, a woman's daughter is using drugs and hanging around with the wrong crowd. This mother may think what she wants is "my daughter to stop using drugs and to stop hanging around with those rotters". But the daughter's decision to use drugs and choose her own friends is the *daughter's* decision and has nothing to do with her mother's wishes.

Here's the more important question: Is her daughter's cessation of drug use and her changing companions what the mother *really* wants? Sure, at one level any mother would want that for a daughter. But wouldn't it be more accurate to say that deep down what the mother really wants is a loving relationship with her daughter? Isn't that essentially what she's looking for? What is stopping her from having one? Her dissatisfaction with her daughter's lifestyle.

Remember, the question is "What do *I* want?" Be sure what you want is not for someone else to change what he or she wants.

List what changes you want to make and then pick the one single statement that best represents this desire.

_____

_____

_____

_____

_____

_____

2 The next question to answer is this:

What is keeping me where I am?

Write as many reasons as you can think of. Why haven't you changed? If your desire to change has been strong enough to lead you to read this book, then why haven't you changed by now? There has to be a reason, or reasons. What's keeping you where you are?

On ancient maps any uncharted land was referred to as *terra incognita*, meaning "unknown region". Dragons and sea monsters were drawn to indicate these places. These monsters were the graphic expression of cartographers' own convictions - that great danger awaited sailors foolish enough to sail into these unknown regions.

Turn-Around

Are you reading a map of your life drawn by someone else? Are you looking at monsters that were put there by unthinking words spoken by parents or siblings or school mates? The geographical lands that were branded *terra incognita* contained rich resources. What is keeping you from exploring more of who *you* are? Write down everything you can think of.

_____

_____

_____

_____

_____

_____

Now select the three main factors.

a) _____

b) _____

c) _____

3 Next, ask yourself: *What will I do that will move me from where I am to where I want to be?*

What *specific* steps can you take to move you from where you are to where you want to be? Make the list as complete as you can. "I'll try harder" is not a *specific* step. You probably have been trying harder but it's not done you that much good. Make a list of *specific* steps you will take to move you toward your goal.

We're talking about "steps" here, not "leaps". Unless you're Superman you don't leap tall buildings in a single bound. You get to the top floor one step at a time. **Now is the time to make a list of everyday things you can do to move you from where you are to where you want to be.**

Turn-Around

Now select the three most important steps you will take.

a) _____

_____

b) _____

_____

c) _____

_____

4 *How will my life look and how will I feel when my goal is reached?*

How will you know when you're getting closer to your destination? How will you know you've arrived? Answering these questions will help you keep your eyes on the prize and will serve to motivate you.

5 Time for the commitment part: *Read your answers daily.*

There's really no point in writing if you are not going to read what you've written. Reading what you want -

your goal - and the measures you will take to get there is one of the best ways to stay committed. Ever wonder why gyms have so many mirrors? It's because we like to see ourselves striving and improving. We like to see our progress, see our bodies change as we work them. It keeps our eyes on the prize.

So read over these answers every morning and every evening, constantly reminding yourself where you are going. *See* your goal clearly and your commitment to reach it will stay fresh.

Accept what you have written here as your solemn commitment to the universe and to yourself.

Turn-Around

Step Four -
DETACH AND AFFIRM

Step Four - DETACH AND AFFIRM

You can't plant a flower on top of a weed.

While it's true that thoughts are the supreme moulders of our world and initiate all changes, something wonderful happens when we translate our thoughts into sentences and speak them. Such words set up potent vibrations in our body. Speaking *and* hearing *and* feeling our thoughts will impress them more fully on us than merely thinking them. Words move us into action. When, by speaking, we declare our thoughts, every atom of our body responds to the sound of our voice. Not only do we *hear* what we say, we actually *feel* what we say.

The intensity of the effect of our words depends on the intensity of the thought and feeling behind them and the way the words are spoken. An obvious example of this is the fact that soothing words create the release of "soothing" chemicals in the body of the listener *and* the speaker. You've probably experienced this when talking to a frightened child and perhaps remember how it felt when you were a child. Angry words, on the other hand, cause the release of harmful "fight or flight" chemicals in both speaker and listener.

Every word we speak is saturated with energy that will create or destroy. We cannot help becoming what we consistently say we are. In a very real way, our word becomes our world. The more resolutely and intensely we speak the words of who and what we are, the more surely we move toward becoming what we say. And if we insist on accepting the words directed at us by others ("Poor Joe, he's always had health problems!" or, "You've never been good at mathematics." or, "You're going back to college? Ha!" or, "Fatso!" or, "Stupid."), then we will move in the direction that their words send us as well.

Our own words affect us the most because the words we use reflect our thoughts about ourselves - and more! They are the very cause of maintaining those thoughts. So if you tell yourself, "You idiot, you messed up again. You're really worthless", you are not only affirming your present sense of worth, you are setting up the parameters of your worth in the future: *Today's words become tomorrow's reality. They can build and they can destroy.*

A "Born-Again" City

"Let's clear away the whole mess!" The city council had had enough of the crime and filth, so in an attempt to reclaim a particular area of the city they decided to tear down their ugly, dangerous slums and demolish all the abandoned buildings, burnt-out homes and tenements. Several blocks were cleared and, after years of having looked like a war zone, it was an amazing improvement.

But then something very unexpected happened. The shacks and rubbish and vagrants started creeping back, and the cleared areas were on their way to being as seedy and undesirable as before.

The council didn't take long to realize it's not enough to *remove* offensive structures. You have to *replace* them with something better. So, after clearing away the sprouting slums a second time, the land was leased out for the construction of a theatre complex, a shopping complex, and office buildings. After that, the slums did not return.

This "born-again" city is a great lesson for us. If we expect to reclaim our souls, we have to get rid of our "ugly and dangerous" beliefs and attitudes. But we quickly have to follow up by replacing the old stuff with new thoughts and attitudes, or else the old will creep back again.

This is why the next *TURN-AROUND* step is to DETACH from your thinking everything not true about your situation and AFFIRM the truth about it. And what is the "truth"? The truth is that you do not have to be buffeted about by the winds of circumstances and events. You can tap your inner wisdom, which is part of the great cosmic mind, and take charge of your life. What seems to be and what actually is are usually separated by a Grand Canyon's worth of faulty assumptions.

DETACH

A series of scientific studies carried out to determine how attitude affects performance was very revealing and quite surprising to those who designed the experiments. In the first experiment, two separate groups of senior citizens were given the same standard memory test. But before the test was administered, one group was shown subliminal messages (words quickly flashed on a monitor without the viewers' being consciously aware of them) containing words like "old", "Alzheimer's", and "senile". The other group was flashed words like "sage" and "wise". The group shown the more positive words scored as much as sixty-five per cent better in the memory test!

In another experiment there was a significant difference in scores of two groups of women taking a mathematics test. The ones who, before the test, had filled out information subtly reminding them of their gender scored much lower than those not reminded at all. The seemingly innocuous act of having to identify themselves as women reminded them of the stereotype that women are not good at mathematics.

Finally, forty black and forty white college students took part in a simplistic psychological test. All the students had to do was merely play miniature golf. Before they played, half of the black and half of the white students were told it was a test of "natural ability". The remaining students were told it was a test to measure "the ability to think strategically". The students then played the course one at a time with some surprising results. In the group told the test measured "natural ability", the black students, on average, scored more than four strokes better than the white students. In the group told the test gauged "the ability to think strategically", the white students scored more than four strokes better!

The psychologists analyzing these three experiments concluded that when people are reminded of a negative stereotype, it can adversely affect their performance.*

Amazing stuff, don't you think? Remember, these people were not consciously aware that deep in their souls they were holding stereotypical images of themselves, yet obviously they were. Whether the cues come from society, our family, the news media,

* *The Stereotype Trap,* NEWSWEEK, November 6, 2000, pp. 66 - 68.

our childhood memories or anywhere else, our closely held (often unconscious) thoughts about ourselves squeeze into every nook and cranny of our lives - from our jobs to our relationships to our own self-image. *We cannot help becoming what we truly believe ourselves to be.*

That's why it's so critical for us to be aware of the messages we are unconsciously accepting and allowing to take root in our souls. And that's why the process of detaching from these stereotypes and affirming our unique and authentic selves is so effective.

What are the hidden thoughts and beliefs about yourself that you've been carrying around for the past few years or maybe even the past few decades? Are they true? Have they served you well? If not, every time they pop into your head as thoughts or images, change them immediately. Replace them with new and improved thoughts and feelings. Dare to become the absolutely unique and authentic individual *you* want to be rather than what your father or mother or husband or wife or children or friends or society says you are. Remember, these messages are subtle. Like parasites they attach themselves to your soul and suck the authenticity out of you. You end up believing what you hear about yourself and so you become it.

Turn-Around

The Power To Eliminate

Isn't it marvellous that we, along with all other forms of life on this planet, have been given the power of elimination! Without elimination we couldn't rid our bodies of the toxic wastes of metabolism. We would have no way of releasing those life-denying poisons that accumulate daily as a result of normal living. But the fact is we are able, through our intestines, kidneys, skin and lungs, to excrete these metabolic wastes. In denying these life-depleting poisons a place in our bodies, we strengthen and support those life-sustaining forces that heal us and keep us well.

Yet the faculty of elimination is not the exclusive purview of our physical bodies. We have the ability to eliminate from our souls as well. We can turn aside from *anything* in our lives that doesn't sustain and nurture us, including worn-out beliefs and habitual thoughts that no longer have meaning in our lives. The following may help to clarify this concept.

Intense summer rains in Alaska make mud highways out of the dirt roads that criss-cross the state. As cars and trucks travel these roads, deep grooves are cut which, when winter arrives, become frozen solid. A sign on one of these roads reads, "Choose your rut carefully. You'll be in it for the next 20 miles."

Thinking the same thoughts and reacting in the same ways cuts "grooves" in our souls. These same old thoughts and same old knee-jerk reactions bind us to the same old outcomes. If we want to change our lives we first have to change our thoughts. (Ultimately, we have to cut a new groove.)

We can make a statement that mirrors our desire to get out of our rut. Such a statement detaches us from the "same old same old" - the same old thoughts leading to the same old results. Whenever those old thoughts enter our heads, we repeat these phrases of detachment to remind ourselves that our former habitual thinking was not entirely on target and that there is a higher, more accurate way of looking at our situation.

Make Them Meaningful To You

Please note that when we detach ourselves from our old way of thinking about our present challenge, we are not denying the challenge exists. We are simply denying this circumstance any power or control over us. (If we truly believe the problem facing us has power over us, then we don't believe there is any power higher than the problem itself!)

We can detach from something most effectively when, in response to a negative thought, our statements are in the form of a simple sentence, said aloud as often as possible until the offending thought is either erased or subdued. Although it is always the thoughts and feelings behind the words that provide the catalyst for soul changes, the words themselves can be a great motivator in helping us. For instance, an alcoholic may want to drink and try to convince his intellect by saying, "I won't take this drink because I don't like alcohol." Yeah, right! This is most certainly untrue. Certainly he likes it, that's why he's been drinking for so long. So he would have a difficult time convincing himself with that statement. It could be more believable and effective for him to say, "I will **NOT** take this drink because I don't *need* it." Sure, he may crave it, but the truth is he doesn't *need* it to survive. Or "I won't take this drink because I want my life to be better." His intellect can agree with those statements and so it is easier for him to plant them into his consciousness, into his soul. By removing the inaccurate belief that his continued drinking is inevitable, he has taken the first step toward freedom from the addiction.

The Positive Power Of "NO!"

Some people don't like to use statements of detachment; they think of them as "too negative" and like to speak only affirmations instead. But affirming the truth without first detaching from the false is like changing a

baby's nappy by putting a clean one over a soiled one!
Detachments, when used properly, are *not* negative.
Their value lies in the use of the POSITIVE power
of "no".

Before any rebuilding can take place in your life
or circumstances, you have to first address whatever is
causing you trouble. If your house were on fire,
wouldn't you first call the fire brigade to put it out
before calling a building contractor to rebuild it? If there
were a disease organism in your body, wouldn't you first
get rid of it *before* choosing a diet and exercise
programme to rebuild your body? In much the same
way, detaching allows you to remove your inaccurate
beliefs as you begin reconstructing your soul.

Can you fill a life with health without eliminating the
thought of sickness? Can you fill a life with love
without getting rid of the hatred? Can a life be filled
with prosperity without detaching from the belief
in a personal poverty? Can you plant a flower on top
of a weed?

Mean What You Say

In "Soul Steps" you'll be creating a detach statement.
When challenged with an old, negative thought that
spontaneously enters your head, repeat this statement as
soon as possible to detach yourself from that thought. It

does not necessarily have to be aloud although, when you do speak it aloud, the louder the better! And whenever you say it, either silently or audibly, say it with *conviction*, with *feeling*. A thought without feeling has no value. It's like dynamite without a match. But when your words are saturated with faith and sincerity and conviction, they are powerful explosives that will shatter the old negative beliefs, clearing the way for the growth of a new, clearer, more positive state of mind.

Do you believe you're too *weak* to stop drinking alcohol? Do you believe you don't have the *smartness* to go back and finish college? Do you believe because the last three generations of your family were poor you *deserve* to be poor? Do you really believe you're *meant* to be sick? Beliefs like these may have been drilled into you (consciously or subconsciously) as a child and you may have accepted them and nurtured them until you see them as a mountain too high to climb. But if you are persistent in consciously detaching from negative thoughts or old, habitual, untrue beliefs as soon as they appear, they will be released from your soul along with the unpleasant conditions they have spawned.

AFFIRM

It's not enough to pull weeds in a garden - flowers must be planted so the weeds will have fewer places to grow. Detaching helps you get rid of wrong beliefs about a situation (weeds), but it must be followed by positive affirmations (flowers) if you're looking for complete success.

An affirmation works on at least two levels. On a psychological level it acts as a means of changing your habitual thinking. This process is known in behavioural psychology as "cognitive restructuring". In other words, you are restructuring or renovating your thinking. You're learning to come to a conclusion by means of a different process than you have used in the past. On this level alone it is a very effective tool.

An affirmation is also a valuable tool on the spiritual level, but here, rather than restructuring, its primary purpose is to increase awareness - your awareness of the presence of an inner wisdom both in the particular situation you are facing and in your life in general.

Like detachments, affirmations should be repeated, either silently or audibly, as often as possible. It's important to remind yourself that your affirmations are not "making something come into existence". When you affirm something, you are acknowledging your inner wisdom and its commitment to working out the right solution.

Look For The Silver Lining

As you're reading this you may be hard-pressed to find something positive in your particular situation. But when in your heart of hearts you truly desire a change, you'll be led to create a detach statement along with a powerful affirmation. It's not important to fully believe your affirmation before you begin using it. The very repetition of it, *if it is true* (note well the phrase "if it is true"), will soon convince you of its truth and you will eventually accept it.

The muscles of a leg that has been in a cast for a long time may be so weakened from lack of use they are unable to move by themselves. But as a therapist coaxes the leg to move, the muscles soon remember their role, slowly gain strength, and before long are able to move on their own. The more they are used, of course, the stronger they become.

So it is with affirmations. You may just be "saying words" with no conviction behind them when you begin. But *if the affirmation is based on truth* - that there is an unseen power at work in this - it will create a momentum of its own and you will finally accept the truth it contains.

Work With Only What's True

Just to recap a bit, both detach statements and affirmations must be firmly anchored in the truth. Something is not false just because you deny it; *you deny it because it is false.* This is a critical distinction and it's important to be clear on the distinction.

Conversely, something is not true just because you affirm it; *you affirm it because it is true.* Here, again, an important distinction.

Something cannot be "detached" out of existence nor "affirmed" into existence. But inaccurate thoughts and feelings about something can be detached, and thoughts and feelings based on the truth can be affirmed.

For example, if all you had in the world were ten pounds in your bank account, how could you deny you were "poor"? How could you say with conviction, "I am *not* poor", when by every economic and financial measurement you are poor? But there would be a deeper truth you could believe and say with conviction, such as, "I may be poor now *but I don't have to stay poor."* Or you could say, "Poverty is NOT my inevitable state in life." You are detaching yourself from the superficial appearance, which can be temporary. You are detaching from the feelings and belief that poverty is inevitable - and that's true. So when you repeat these kinds of statements you are making it easier to turn your back on the thoughts of a life continuing to be lived in poverty.

Continuing with our example, an appropriate affirmation would *not* be, "I have loads of money", because, in fact, you have only ten pounds to your name. But you could rightfully affirm that as an integral part of an abundant universe you have the potential for unlimited wealth. "All my needs will be met." Or, "I have access to ideas I can use to create prosperity."

Detach and Affirm then is the fourth step of *TURN-AROUND*. The technique of Detach and Affirm is so basic and deceptively simple that it is easy to disregard it, forgetting how effective it can be.

Detaching is a tearing-down process - it pulls up weeds. Detach statements remove the negative beliefs from your soul, those beliefs and ideas and attitudes, often from childhood, not based on the truth of things. Detach yourself from these outdated beliefs and they will gradually fade away. If a weed gets no nourishment, it withers and dies.

Affirmations are a building-up process - they plant flowers. Affirmations construct and implant the positive aspects in your soul, those beliefs and ideas and attitudes based on what is true about you.

Taken together, these techniques are a powerful tool for turning your life around.

Turn-Around

Detach and Affirm - SOUL STEPS

Detach and Affirm - SOUL STEPS

You can read people's minds simply by listening to their words! In fact, that's the purpose of speaking - to let someone else know what you're thinking about a particular subject.

In exactly the same way, you can read your own mind, check on your own soul, if you listen to your words. Your fears, your worries, your desires, your hopes and dreams, your loves, are all expressed through the words you speak. If you listen very carefully to your words, you'll find out a lot about yourself because your words are actually your distilled thoughts and feelings.

Since your words reflect your thoughts, it follows that as you change your thoughts you'll change your words. What is equally true but does not seem as logical is that this also works in reverse. Strange as it sounds, as you consciously change your *words,* your thoughts and feelings will change to reflect them!

The brain doesn't know the difference between something real and something vividly imagined. Because of the brain's inclination to accept a vividly imagined thought as real, you can talk yourself into a different way of thinking and feeling. That's because when you speak a word, you send a signal through a neural pathway, you "cut a groove" in the brain. The more you use this "groove", the more pronounced it gets, and the more easily your thoughts and feelings will follow this groove. (Think frozen roads in Alaska.) So if you regularly affirm, "I can have a loving relationship with my son", in the face of his long-standing hostility towards you, *your* soul will actually change. Before long you will believe that it can be done. Once you are convinced, your every word will mirror this change of attitude, and your actions have no choice but to follow. Remember the analogy of the gears in the "Blessing" chapter and how changing only one gear will change the final outcome? Well, your thoughts and emotions are a HUGE gear in any situation you find yourself in. If you can change your thinking and feelings about something, how that something affects you will definitely change too.

"YES" And "NO"

Now it's your turn to create your own detachments and affirmations, your own tools for releasing the negative beliefs and accepting the true ones. One good, strong detachment statement and one powerful affirmation, both based on the essential truth, is all you really need - ones that can be easily memorized and called upon throughout the day when needed.

Make your statements short and use vivid, descriptive words. Be original and personal. Once in a while you may find someone else's statements strike a responsive chord in you, but since they must have strong meaning for you in order to be effective, usually the statements you yourself create are more meaningful and therefore more powerful. They must have strong meaning for *you* in order to be effective.

Begin by creating some detach statements. Remember, you're trying to break up the old thinking that is thick with the accumulation of years of hardened belief about your situation. Encrusted thoughts and emotions demand powerful, very pointed statements to break them up. The best tool for breaking up hardened concrete is a pickaxe. This sharply pointed tool puts the maximum amount of pressure on the smallest area, breaking up the hardened material much more quickly than a broad-faced hammer could ever do.

Likewise with your statement of detachment. A short, very pointed, sharply directed statement *proclaimed with passion* has a powerful impact on your thought patterns, especially when backed by your conviction and emotion.

One of the best detach statements is the simplest one: *"NO!"* Spoken with conviction (and preferably a loud voice!) when a negative thought or image ambushes you, "NO!" blasts it out of there. A sharp **"NO"** is a terrific tool to use when a destructive thought or emotion insists on crashing the party and hanging out in your soul.

Conversely, *"YES"* is a great affirmation following a spontaneous, positive thought or image. When you want to reinforce something positive - maybe an event or maybe simply your own feelings - give it a powerful "YES!"

YES and NO are *re*active statements. They are used only in response to a spontaneous thought and/or event. But a simple "NO" may not be enough. There may be a real need for a specific statement of detachment to be repeated any time a negative thought enters your mind throughout the day.

1 **Create three strong, true and meaningful detach statements appropriate to your situation.** Use these in response to any negative thought about your situation that appears in your mind. For example:

I do NOT accept poverty.

I don't want poverty in my life any more.

Poverty stinks. I'm through with it.

If you're not satisfied with your health, try something like:

I do NOT accept poor health.

I will NOT allow sickness in my life any more.

No more sickness!

Turn-Around

Your list of detach statements:

a) _____

_____

b) _____

_____

c) _____

_____

While it's a good idea to repeat affirmations *pro*actively throughout the day, it normally is NOT a good idea to do the same with your detach statements. Statements of detachment are best used only when you're aware that a negative thought or feeling has entered your mind, in other words, *re*actively. If there is no negative thought about your present challenge in your mind, there's no reason to remind yourself that you have one - best to let sleeping dogs lie. If detach statements are used consistently whenever a negative thought enters your mind, these negative thoughts will stop bubbling up. After all, if you stopped answering the telephone, people would stop calling. It's the same with thoughts and emotions - the unwelcome ones stop showing up.

2 As we've said, "YES" is a terrific reactive statement and is best used when a spontaneous positive thought about your present challenge pops into your head. But it's not enough to wait for a positive thought to drift by and then nurture it. *Pro*active, positive statements concerning your challenge need to be repeated regularly throughout the day.

Create three powerful, true and positive affirmations appropriate to your situation. For example:

I am ready to be prosperous.
I'm on my way to prosperity.
Prosperity, here I come!

If your challenge is in the area of health, you could affirm something like the following:

I am ready to be well.
I'm on my way to better health.
I am healed.

Your list of affirmations:

a) _____

b) _____

_____

c) _____

_____

3 Select the one detach statement and the one affirmation that has the most meaning for you.

Choose a detach statement that best cancels out the negative image you have of your challenge - the one destructive thought or feeling most consistently bubbling up into your mind.

a) **My detach statement is:**

_____

_____

_____

Choose the affirmation that best describes how you want to feel.

b) **My affirmation is:**

_____

_____

_____

4 Memorize them both.

5 Either say "NO" or repeat your detach statement *every time* **a negative image of your challenge appears in your mind -** *EVERY TIME!*

6 Repeat your affirmation often - silently or audibly throughout the day until it becomes so much a part of you that it springs to mind automatically. And constantly in your mind is exactly where you want it, because that's where it will do its most powerful work.

Turn-Around

Step Five -
ENERGIZE IT

Step Five - ENERGIZE IT

There are two ways to get to the top of an oak tree. You can climb to the top or you can sit on an acorn and wait.

The biggest challenge with humans living in space and the one not yet overcome is what happens when the body is in a weightless environment for too long. Apparently when the body doesn't have to make the effort to overcome gravity, the muscles lose strength and the bones lose calcium and other minerals. One astronaut who was in space for four months said it took him over a year to gain back all of his strength in spite of working out on special exercise machines every day while in space. It seems the effort needed to move the body in space is a whole lot less than the body's design calls for. We thrive on effort.

Every step of *TURN-AROUND* so far has been involved with consciousness - with your thinking and feeling faculties. This is as it should be. All things begin in the mind, with ideas and beliefs. You have become AWARE of exactly what your challenge is and perhaps even of the underlying cause of it. You are able to BLESS the situation because it contains the seed of something positive. You made a solemn COMMITMENT with universal intelligence that is motivating you toward achieving your goal. And you are using those uncanny soul conditioners, DETACH AND AFFIRM, to bring about a shift in your consciousness. *Now is the time to take action* - time to bring the new ideas and new attitudes out into the physical world. And the only way you can do this is by making an effort, a genuine effort, on your own behalf.

Wheat kernels found in an Egyptian tomb many thousands of years old were still capable of growing. It was estimated that if they had been planted and their seeds replanted from then until now, those few original seeds would have yielded enough wheat to feed the entire world. *But nobody planted them!*

Like the wheat kernels in the tomb - rich in potential but poor in actual yield - thoughts, too, will lie fallow when not translated into action. Thoughts or desires are powerful, but they must be energized, converted into action, in order to reach their full potential.

Without effort, all of the groundwork you've laid up to this point will accomplish little or nothing. No matter how sincere or extensive your first four steps of *TURN-AROUND* might be, if you don't energize them with a dedicated effort, they cannot be successful. The degree of your own inner conviction will reflect in the degree of effort you are now willing to put forth. *Your effort actually becomes the tangible proof of your inner dedication.* It is your outward indication to the universe that you believe in yourself and that you are in synch with your inner wisdom.

Physicians often report that some people hope to be healed so they can continue to live in the same manner as before, which of course doesn't work. (The manner in which they were living is usually what got them into trouble in the first place.) In fact, a surprisingly high percentage of heart bypass patients have chosen the surgery rather than earlier opting to change their unhealthy lifestyle. Old habits are very comfortable. To put forth the energy to break these habits is often more than some of us are willing to do, so we convince ourselves the problem can be solved by merely "affirming my good" or "praying for deliverance". We are often able to rationalize away the most convincing evidence, knowingly break the laws of health, and then expect divine intervention when we refuse to make any effort to help ourselves! A diabetic keeps on eating foods she knows are harmful, a recovering heart patient refuses to do the exercises his physician suggested, an obese person continues to reach for second helpings, a recovering alcoholic stops going to meetings. Do these acts make sense?

Are these people really putting forth an effort on their own behalf?

A Desire Needs A Deed

The crux of the matter is this: *a desire without a deed is a dead end.* No matter how strong our desires, unless we energize our desire by making an effort on our own behalf we cannot expect improvement. That would be looking for a free lunch - expecting something for nothing. To believe some mysterious force is going to intervene and bring us health or love or prosperity after we have disregarded the orderly laws of the universe is futile and irrational and potentially perilous. Is it rational to believe we can pray to keep emphysema away if we keep smoking cigarettes? Is it logical to want the love of that certain special person if we continue to hate a certain someone else? Do we really believe we can pray money into our pockets if we won't even look for a job? Your success starts when you start.

Let's say you are dealing with a difficult relationship. Although the effort involved in loving someone whom you hate and whom you feel hates you rests purely within your own soul, it may be an extraordinarily difficult thing for you to do. You may have completed all of the other steps of *TURN-AROUND* but your awareness, blessing, commitment, detachments and affirmations are useless unless they act as catalysts to energize you to make an *effort* to forgive and to love. Without effort your world will exist in the darkness of hatred and resentment, and your true potential will stay cowering in a shadowy corner, hidden from your own and everyone else's view. But if you make the *effort* to love, if you energize the infinite potential of love lying dormant in you, if you do your best to love, then love becomes the great emancipator, freeing you to become aware of and activate the incredible possibilities within you.

Forgive Your Enemy

So often the need for a healing in our bodies or affairs is linked to an unwillingness to love or forgive. That is why our greatest teachers are those people whom we hate or dislike or who oppose us in some way - they give us the opportunity to see our weaknesses. The oil gauge light that blinks on your dashboard shows you have an oil leak in your car, yet you don't hate the oil gauge! No, you are thankful for having something that shows you where your car needs attention. And like the blinking oil gauge, those we regard as "enemies" can teach us the most about ourselves because they reflect back to us something in ourselves that needs our attention.

Let's face it, harbouring resentments toward someone doesn't hurt that person, it hurts you. In fact, your
"enemies" often don't even know they are hated or
resented, so how can it hurt them? But it fills your soul
with bitterness and, wherever there is bitterness, the
healing flow of love is dammed up.

Imagine this. Your bank is having a "FREE GOLD
COINS GIVEAWAY DAY" but you have to bring your
own bag. Are you going to bring a bag filled with junk?
No way! You would be sure the bag was empty so every
cubic inch of it could hold as many gold coins as
possible. In the same sense, why cram your soul with the
junk of hatred and unforgiveness when it can be filled
with the most wonderful coin of the realm - love?

A friend of ours went through a bitter divorce,
during which her former husband moved a continent
away to be with his new girlfriend. Every time our
friend remembers him she thinks "Over there on the
sunny riviera with his bimbo while I'm stuck here in this
dismal office, I hate him". Does this really make
sense? He's miles away having a great time, oblivious
to her episodes of churning out hatred toward
him. Even if he did know, it would not affect him.
But imagine the unbelievable harm she is doing
to herself! Mix hurt with a heavy helping of hate
and you invariably conjure up something so toxic

to the body and soul it should have a skull and crossbones on it!

Are You Willing?

When things go wrong in your life, don't go wrong with them. You have been given the unconditional gift of free will. You are personally in charge of your own life. That's the good news. What may seem like not so good news is that this means your destiny is always in your own hands. But that's actually good news too because it means every time you make a genuine effort to improve your life, every time you really try to express all that you are, you actually align yourself with the great power that runs this universe. Your sincere effort automatically puts you in the flow of this power.

Turn-Around

Energize It - SOUL STEPS

Energize It - SOUL STEPS

The best designed, sleekest, and most powerful rocket in the world is a helpless pile of metal, wires, and fuel until a battery energizes it. Only then can it soar beyond the clouds.

The most beautiful blueprint of a home is a series of lifeless pencil lines until someone puts the energy into making the plans come to life.

Put another way, there are two ways to get to the top of an oak tree:

1 You can climb to the top.

2 You can sit on an acorn and wait.

Are you climbing or are you waiting?

1 Review the list of promises in your commitment. (See SOUL STEPS in Step Three.)

a) Do you still feel they are a valid way of overcoming your situation? Scrutinize the steps. Are they the best course of action for *all* involved?

b) Are they specific? It may not be enough merely to promise to accept a troublesome neighbour. A more specific act would be to invite her over for lunch or to make some other overt act of kindness toward her. Even waving to her or smiling as you drive by her in your car is a specific step. A positive action will begin to convince not only your neighbour but also you, yourself, of the depth of your commitment to establishing an amicable relationship. (Remember, only one gear has to change in order for all gears to change!)

c) Lastly, and most importantly, are you following the promises of your commitment? Regularity is the key. Half-hearted effort can only deliver half-hearted results.

2 **Meditate daily.** This keeps you in touch with your inner awareness, providing you with constant guidance in your efforts and adjusting your programme as your situation improves.

3 Barnacles are a problem for all seagoing vessels. These small creatures firmly attach themselves to the hulls of boats. The sheer number of them adds weight and increases turbulence, slowing down the speed and manoeuvreability of the boats. As they grow larger and increase in number, the boat is less and less able to perform normally. If allowed to accumulate the barnacles will render the boat completely unable to function. And so a boat must be periodically taken out of the water and the barnacles scraped off.

As we "sail" through life we acquire "barnacles". They are the resentments and hatreds and unforgiveness that mentally and spiritually "weigh us down" and increase the amount of turbulence in our lives.

Turn-Around

We (the authors) are convinced the single most consequential effort you can make in your life is to forgive everyone and anyone whom you are now judging to be unworthy of your love. Every hateful thought and every unkind word directed toward another person becomes a "barnacle" attached to your soul. Every time you entertain such feelings you attach another one. Such feelings weigh you down and render you unable to express the unconditional love that is so crucial to your soul growth.

Since love and forgiveness are key factors in your *TURN-AROUND*, **you are going to work now on identifying and releasing any resentment and bitterness you may have buried in your heart.** This has to happen before you can progress any further in healing what needs to be healed.

Granted, the situation often seems "too big" to forgive. *"I can never forgive him - ever - for what he did."* Or, *"Well, maybe I'll forgive him but I certainly won't forget it."* That's not real forgiveness, and so it's not going to work. What you do in this case is get it in your heart and soul that you at least want to forgive. *"I don't know how this can ever happen, considering what he did. But I know that for the sake of my own soul, I should forgive. So, yes, I am* willing *to forgive."* And, incredibly, the willingness is enough to begin the process and make it happen.

It's like isometric exercises, the body-building technique where muscles strain to move immoveable objects. Although there is no visible movement, the muscles still strengthen and develop because they are being challenged. Same with forgiveness. If you can't yet forgive, the mere desire, the *wanting to forgive*, is enough to build your "forgiveness muscle" and bring true forgiveness that much closer.

Unforgiveness stands directly in the way of unconditional love. There's no way we can really love until we forgive. All of the great religions admonish us to "love your enemy". Why? Because *the power inherent in our divinity is available to us only when we love.* (Another phrase worth repeating - so we will: *the power inherent in our divinity is available to us only when we love.*) If we allow someone, anyone, to bully us into not loving him or her, we have allowed that person to take our power. The decision to love is too important to relinquish to someone else, but that's exactly what we do when we resent or hate. We wouldn't ever consider giving any of our monetary fortune to someone we did not like yet we give away a veritable treasure when we hate.

Hatred is a jail that imprisons those who hate. The only way to escape is to love your way out.

Your assignment, therefore, is an important one and a tough one. It will take honest and courageous introspection but the rewards will be great. Your assignment is to **make a list of any resentment and/or bitterness you have buried in your heart.**

_____

_____

_____

_____

_____

_____

_____

_____

_____

4 Get started right NOW to release them. Don't wait another day!

Turn-Around

Step Six - FAITH

Step Six - FAITH

We all have unlimited faith, but it's how we invest our faith that makes a difference.

A famous medical case involves a man with a virulent form of cancer - lymphosarcoma. Gravely ill, he had huge tumour masses and needed fluid drained from his chest every other day. Frequently he required oxygen and could do little but lie in bed. His physician was at that time involved in cancer research on a promising new drug. Upon hearing about the drug and everyone's high expectations of it, the man begged to be treated with it. With nothing to lose, his physician complied. The man made a "startling" recovery - his tumours disappeared, his chest stopped filling with fluid, he no longer needed extra oxygen, he got out of bed, and he even began flying his private aeroplane again.

He was symptom-free for two months at which point some negative publicity about the drug began to appear. The news media published reports about the failure of the drug in some preliminary tests. Almost at once the man's symptoms began reappearing. Before long he again experienced the massive tumours, the fluid-filled chest and the need for extra oxygen. He became bedridden and unable to work.

His physician, observing this rapid decline and daring to follow his intuition, informed the man of a new, improved, super-strength batch of the drug far superior to the former one and that he wanted to administer it to him. The man enthusiastically agreed and the new injections were initiated. This time, however, the injections were not the drug at all - they were merely *sterile water.*

Yet once again the man made "remarkable" improvement. The tumour masses melted, there was no more fluid in the chest, no need for the oxygen mask. The man returned to work and once more began to fly his aeroplane.

But within a short time, newspaper headlines proclaimed the news that the drug had proven worthless in the treatment of cancer. A few days after reading this news the man was dead.

A "Hopeless" Case

Contrast that case with a case observed and recorded by the great Nobel prizewinning physician, Alexis Carrel, and later described in his inspiring book *The Voyage To Lourdes* (Harper & Brothers, New York, 1950). As a young physician Dr Carrel travelled with a trainload of sick to the shrine at Lourdes, France, his intention being to learn whether the reports of radical improvements from Lourdes were authentic. During the train trip some of the faithful were so ill that Dr Carrel was frequently called to attend to them. He was kept especially busy with a patient named Marie, a young girl with what Carrel described as "a classic case of tubercular peritonitis". Suffering with this condition for eight months, she was so ill and her condition so precarious that her personal physician had refused to operate on her, considering her case "hopeless".

While on the train to Lourdes, Marie lapsed into a coma several times and it was only Dr Carrel's medical intervention that saved her. In talking with the girl (and later with her personal physician at home) Dr Carrel learned that both of her parents had died of tuberculosis. At seventeen, she was already spitting blood and at eighteen she had a tubercular pleurisy that required more than half a gallon of fluid to be drawn from her left lung. She had pulmonary lesions and for the last eight months had an unmistakable tubercular peritonitis.

Nevertheless, Marie insisted on being taken to Lourdes. The pain she had to endure on the bumpy train ride was excruciating, but her faith was so strong she gladly bore it.

After arriving at Lourdes, Carrel was called again to minister to the girl. This time he brought another physician with him to examine her. They both agreed, "She is almost completely wasted away. Her heart is racing madly (one hundred and fifty beats per minute and irregular). Look how thin she is. Look at the colour of her face and hands. She may last a few more days, but she is doomed. Death is very near." Carrel felt, "She may die any moment right under my nose. If she gets home again alive, that in itself will be a miracle."

Marie was resolute in her desire to be bathed in the water at Lourdes. Her abdomen was so sore and her body so frail it was decided not to immerse her but instead pour the water over her abdomen. Dr Carrel describes the girl: "She lay on her back, all shrunken beneath the dark brown blanket which made a mound over her distended abdomen. Her breath came quick and short. The sick girl was apparently unconscious. Her pulse was more rapid than ever. Her face was ashen. It was obvious that this young girl was about to die."

But the girl did not die. In a matter of two hours after having the water poured over her, Marie had lost all symptoms of her sickness. Dr Carrel reported: "She was cured. In the span of a few hours, a girl with a face already turning blue, a distended abdomen, and a fatally racing heart had been restored...to health."

Turn-Around

Faith Is The Mould

We all have unlimited faith, but it's how we invest our faith that makes the difference. Faith can be invested in sickness or it can be invested in health, it can be invested in hatred or it can be invested in love, it can be invested in poverty or it can be invested in prosperity. *We* choose what fills our lives, and faith is the mould into which it is poured. Faith shapes the results we get. If someone's faith is shaped in the expectation of wholeness and health, guess what pours itself into the mould?

Underlying almost every step of *TURN-AROUND* is FAITH. Without at least a smidgen of faith in your eventual success you would never have achieved an AWARENESS of the situation nor dared to BLESS it. It certainly would have been foolish to make a COMMITMENT to overcoming the situation if you had no faith in your ability to do so. The same holds true for DETACH and AFFIRM - why waste time in detaching and affirming if you have no faith in a positive outcome? And some degree of faith is necessary if you are going to make any meaningful EFFORT on our own behalf. (Who would ever expend any effort on what he or she regarded as a hopeless situation?) Maybe you didn't feel any faith when you began, but there has to be some or you would have given up trying to change, simply accepting suffering as inevitable and immutable.

Two Faiths

Let's return to our two extraordinary examples of faith, both of which are authentic cases, by the way.

The cancer patient had a faith that was purely an intellectual faith based *totally* on an appearance. Even after being given the drug and becoming symptom-free for two months (!), his faith could not resist the negative reports of the news media. Then, in a heroic effort the life force within him made him healthy a second time - this time without any help from a drug! But he could not accept even the evidence of his own healed body as proof of his health. Sadly, so strongly was his faith attached to outer appearances that he allowed news of the drug's failure to kill him.

Where had this man invested his faith? What was the mould his faith had created to be filled? Was it a deep inner faith that *expected* his body to regain its wholeness and trusted the healing forces within him, or was it an intellectual faith based only on what he could read and hear? An extremely powerful example of a strong faith - but in what?

Marie's faith, on the other hand, allowed her to be healed. The mould created by her faith was the unshakable expectation of wholeness, and was activated deep within her soul. Faith is subject to the law of mind action, which dictates that like attracts like, like begets like. That's why faith as positive and as tenacious as Marie's goes about its work to create a result that can seem miraculous.

Such "miracles" are impossible with intellectual faith alone because the foundation of intellectual faith is on the shifting sands of appearances. When appearances change, faith shifts, and everything built on such faith crumbles.

Marie had faith that when she was bathed with the "holy water" she would get well. True, there was an element of intellectual faith in this since Marie believed the water was necessary for her to be healed. But Marie's faith went much deeper than an intellectual faith in any water. After all, Marie was well aware that the vast majority of people who go to Lourdes are not cured. And at some point, she had to be aware that virtually everyone else who was bathed in the water with her showed no improvement! Yet this mattered not to her. Imagine the deep, solid, strongly rooted faith this girl must have had, knowing of such failures and not being swayed. Had her faith been only an intellectual faith based solely on appearances, it would have crumbled when faced with such overwhelming evidence of failure. But Marie's faith did not falter. The water was merely a catalyst that activated a deeper, more spiritual faith. Marie had absolute trust in her eventual healing - she expected it. This is true faith.

To all outward appearances Marie was fatally ill and her *faith made her well.* To all outward appearances the man was well and *his faith made him fatally ill!*

Turn-Around

Faith -
SOUL STEPS

Faith - SOUL STEPS

Faith is always tethered to an emotion. In fact, faith without an emotion is hollow and worthless - at best, a hope. The problem is, it's just as easy to attach faith to a negative emotion as it is to a positive one. Believing in the negative, expecting the worse, makes for a really powerful faith - especially since society seems to support the negative so much more than the positive.

Psychosomatic illness - the ability of the mind to make a healthy body sick - is an example of negative faith and is a generally accepted phenomenon in the medical community. If we can believe in psychosomatic illness, why is it so difficult to believe in psychosomatic health? If the mind can make a healthy body sick, cannot a mind make a sick body well? The success of placebos certainly indicates that it can.

1 Faith is like play-dough - you can shape it any way you choose. For instance, fear is faith pointed in the wrong direction. Want to know in what direction your faith is pointing? Want to know how strong your faith is? Check out your feelings. **What does your "gut" tell you when you think about the challenge you are facing?** Feelings don't lie. Next time you think of your challenge, pay attention to your gut feeling. That's the

direction your faith is pointing. Get your thoughts together and write a few sentences that sum up what your gut is telling you.

_____

_____

_____

_____

_____

2 **Consciously redirect your faith.** Move it immediately back to where the truth of things lies - to the invisible source - whenever you catch it going in the wrong direction. The more you work at doing this, the easier it becomes. (Hint: Your affirmations can be of great help in accomplishing this.)

3 *Continuously* **be on guard. Watch for any signs indicating you are misdirecting your faith.**
   a) Do you have fears, doubts, and worries about the outcome of your situation?
   b) Do you often discuss your situation with others?
   c) Do you say things like *"my* arthritis", or "I'll

never be able to afford that", or "If only John would see how he is ruining his life"?

These are signs of misplaced faith. They are signals to you to point your faith in a different direction.

Each evening take a mental tally of your faith investments for the day. Were most of them on the positive side or were more on the negative side? Add them up and see which side has the larger total.

What is your score? Do the daily totals indicate your faith is invested in fear or in God?

Your assignment is to work at improving your score.

Turn-Around

Step Seven -
GET OUT OF THE WAY

Step Seven - GET OUT OF THE WAY

There is nothing more to get, only to be.

The trapeze "flyer" swings back and forth in huge arcs high above the sawdust floor of the circus ring. All eyes are upon him as they wait for him to perform his new act. Opposite the flyer, swinging patiently, is his catcher, eager to do his part in making the performance a success. Everything is ready. The flyer has put great effort into practising and expresses faith - by literally putting himself in the hands of his catcher - that the catcher will be at the precise place at the precise time to catch him and not drop him. Obviously the next step for the flyer is to let go of his trapeze bar. Until he does, he cannot reach his goal. Meanwhile, the catcher has been waiting...waiting, but the flyer continues swinging back and forth, clinging to his trapeze!

Let It Go And Let It Grow

Release is essential for completion, and the release must be *total*. The flyer cannot put half his trust in his trapeze and the other half in the catcher. He cannot grab one of the catcher's hands while holding onto his own trapeze with the other! No, the flyer can reach his goal only by showing faith in his catcher, *totally* letting go of his own bar.

Like navigating a river, we make the most progress when we paddle with the flow. Getting out of the way means letting go. It means going with the flow. Does getting out of the way mean you stop trying? No, it means you stop meddling! Does a farmer, after preparing the soil and planting the seed, then turn right around and dig it up every day to see if it is growing? A farmer doesn't need to dig up the seed, but he does need to water and fertilize and weed and generally care for the seed. His responsibility is to nurture the seed, nature's responsibility is to sprout it.

Your first six steps "prepared the soil and planted the seed" of your success, and while now it's time to nurture it, this is also the time to "let it grow". How heartening to know that by turning your situation - your *life* - over to the cosmic mind, you don't have to be concerned with every detail of how things are going to work out for you. The exhausting need to manipulate other people and the pressure to control events is no longer necessary. Changes can take place all around you, and they will merely be experiences to learn or grow from.

And The Answer Is...

Whatever the question, placing your trust in your inner wisdom is the answer. No matter what steps you took or how you used them, you cannot get the most out of your life without taking the final step of getting out of the way so a higher power can do its work freely.

That's the ultimate promise of *TURN-AROUND*. At its most basic level, the steps are designed to remove the obstacles that block your awareness of the presence of a power greater, more infinite, than your human mind. Once you begin removing these obstacles, your life will change - count on it.

In order to help solidify the point we are trying to make, let's talk for a moment about metals and electricity. Silver is the best conductor of electricity. Why? Because, of all the metals, silver is the least resistant to the flow of electricity and, because of this, it yields the least heat and the least waste while allowing the highest flow of electricity to pass through.

What about iron? Iron can conduct electricity. The problem with iron is that it is highly resistant to the flow of electricity and therefore wastes great amounts of electrical energy as heat. Very little electricity gets through.

Quite an obvious lesson on non-resistance, don't you think? Get yourself out of the way. Get rid of the harmful habits, the destructive reactions, the negative ways of looking at things - all the old "stinkin' thinkin'" - so that the activity of spirit can work unimpeded through you to affect your life in a more positive way.

But it is worth repeating once again that when you get out of the way and surrender your situation to your inner wisdom, you don't take that as a signal to give up on your efforts. Not at all. If you were sailing a boat, you would rely on the wind but would still adjust the sails and turn the rudder and do everything necessary to keep the boat moving with the wind. It's no different with steering your life. Continue doing all you can on your own behalf but stay tuned into that infinite source of inspiration and allow it to work freely as it sees fit. You continue releasing your concern but *without relinquishing your efforts or your work with the other steps.*

(Keep in mind that while the path you have chosen for now will lead you to the healing or the prosperity or the relationship or whatever it is you are seeking, the *direction* is always toward more of an awareness of a higher power in your life.)

"Are We There Yet?"

What little child has not asked this question midway through a long car ride? Time limits may be okay for car trips, but be scrupulously careful not to put a time limit on your soul work. The time required for your situation to change is not your concern - something higher is in control of the process, so just let it happen. When you find yourself growing impatient or depressed over the time this is taking, for heaven's sake force yourself to get out of the way...and to trust. If you really want a higher power to take charge of your life, by all means keep working on your own behalf. Only do it with an attitude of trust - of getting out of the way by letting go of doubts, anxieties, worries and fear. Sure, it's tough to control your thoughts and emotions, a bit like trying to keep a colony of swarming ants off your picnic table. But you can do it. How? Just in the way you control the ants. Be on the lookout for them, and when the destructive creatures show up, brush them away!

Remember the example of a rung ladder. You can never reach up to a higher rung of a ladder until you first let go of the lower one. You can never reach up to your blessings unless you first let go of your difficulties. If you have taken the first six steps of *TURN-AROUND* and are still swinging back and forth like the trapeze flyer afraid to let go, make the decision right now to release the situation and put yourself in the mighty hands that support the universe. Become aware that as you are moving toward the solution the solution is moving toward you. And you can feel good about that.

Trusting in the creative process at work in the universe, you are now able to give up the struggle of arranging the world to suit *you*. You realize the answers to all questions are within you as an inner wisdom. There is nothing more to get, only to *be*.

Turn-Around

Get Out of the Way - SOUL STEPS

Turn-Around

Get Out of the Way - SOUL STEPS

If you've ever had a car that didn't start, you know how frustrating it can be - especially if you know nothing about cars. You keep turning the key and pumping the accelerator but still nothing happens. So you open the bonnet to make sure there are no wildly sparking wires swinging about that you can reconnect or no stray cats trying to stay warm. But if everything seems in order and still the car won't start, what do you do? You call a mechanic, of course. And when the mechanic comes, do you tell him what to do? Do you get in his way? Do you start pulling out spark plugs or draining oil or taking things apart or disconnecting wires? Not if you want your car to start you don't. After all, you did everything you could do and it wasn't enough. Now it's time to get out of the way and put yourself in the hands of a professional.

1 Have you imposed a time limit on the resolution of this situation? If so, it's a sure sign you haven't released the outcome.

When speaking or thinking about your challenge, what words and thoughts do you consistently use? Do they indicate that you have imposed a time limit?

_____

_____

_____

_____

_____

_____

_____

_____

_____

2 **Are you able to say with deep feeling, "I'm thankful for all my blessings", even if you may not yet be seeing any blessings?** When the answer is "yes" you have moved yourself out of the way and have released the situation to universal mind, where all solutions are to be found.

Turn-Around

A New Horizon

A NEW HORIZON

There is a greater order to things than you are aware of - you can be sure of this. By not attempting to predict outcomes, by not fretting about your means of getting there, you smooth the way for the plan to reveal itself easily and quickly. Your part is to keep focused on your role and to trust, simply trust.

The outcome? Always as good as or better (and usually different) than what you'd expected or hoped. And looking at the "big picture" of your life, you see that each episode along the way, no matter how difficult at the time, has proven to be a stepping-stone to something even greater. Out of every twist and turn you've been led further along the pathway to a more satisfying - a more *spiritually attuned* - life.

There is always a perfect solution underlying every challenging situation. No matter how far you may have strayed from the awareness of the presence of the guiding force of life, it is ready to show you a direct route back to where your happiness lies. You can walk sure-footedly because the way is prepared before you, and everything - *everything* - will be all right.

Good luck to you, friend. Thank you for joining us in this powerful process. Our warmest blessings are with you.

Richard and Mary-Alice Jafolla

Turn-Around

Index

Turn-Around